WISE SAYINGS FOR BOYS AND GIRLS

by

Adebisi T'Olu. Aromolaran

Illustrations and cover design by
Yvonne Browne

Meroe Publishing Company
P.O. Box 3268
Berkeley, CA 94703

Copyright © 1993 by Adebisi T'Olu. Aromolaran

ISBN 0-9635862-0-3

Meroe Publishing Company
P.O. Box 3268
Berkeley, CA 94703

Dedication

Dedicated to all growing children and students, the scarcest resources of our changing world, and to the millions of parents, teachers, counselors, etc. who are doing everything possible to leave society's imprint on the young people in their care.

ACKNOWLEDGEMENTS

The author wishes to acknowledge with gratitude the contributions of writers, artists, philosophers—living and dead—whose influence is quite visible in a work of this type. Writers and artists impact their community in special ways in every culture.

Among the writers, artists, and philosophers are: Shakespeare, Milton, Pope, Wordsworth, Marx, etc. I am also indebted to Chief J. O. Ajibola's "Owe Yoruba" (Yoruba Proverbs) as well as to the English Bible. I have slightly paraphrased items copyrighted by Mr. Greenwald. I am grateful that he lets me use some of his materials in this little book.

Some other people have offered advice that has helped me in accomplishing this task; among them are Adenrele Iposu, Sikiru Adepoju and a host of others too numerous to mention.

I have made up a significant portion of the materials in WISE SAYINGS. Indirectly, however, I acknowledge all my teachers, the men and the women who have left their impact on me. I'm here using the term 'teachers' generically to include teachers in formal and informal situations of interpersonal exchanges. In this category, also, falls friends and acquaintances from whom I have learned so I can share and teach.

Lastly, I acknowledge the contributions of a set of parents/educators, among them, Ishmael Reed, Valerie Thomas, Lila Jacobs and Bobbie D. Watson, who offered valuable suggestions for the improvement of the text.

Contents

Preface 1

Section 1: Advice 13

Section 2: Philosophy 31

Section 3: Thought-Provoking 43

Section 4: Other 65

Notes 83

Index 89

PREFACE

WISE SAYINGS FOR BOYS AND GIRLS is an unusual book: it is designed as a companion handbook for all those who have the responsibilities for raising society's children. Fortunately, it is not a book about the three R's—reading, writing and arithmetic. It is a book for parents, teachers, preachers, social workers, youth counselors, etc., on the one hand, and young people who can read the printed word on the other. Even when children cannot read, they can listen: they can listen to the wisdom of the ages and ask innumerable questions of parents, teachers, youth counselors and all.

WHY THIS BOOK?

Apparently, there is a time for everything under the sun. It appears this is the time for such a book as this—*WISE SAYINGS FOR BOYS AND GIRLS*. There is a Yoruba proverb which says "Omo l'ere aye.", meaning "children are an inheritance of the earth." ('Yoruba' is the language spoken by the Yoruba people of Nigeria, Africa's largest ethnic group.) If that proverb carries a positive and universal message, I consider it my duty to make a contribution to the process of the socialization of young people and the re-socialization of others.

First, children are generally born into a primary group, the family, where parents and guardians raise them the best way they know. But, families are undergoing changes everywhere while more and more young people are running afoul of the law.

Statistics shows that over seventy per cent of young people

polled complain of boredom. It is known that people who are bored are capable of many deviant behaviors; they are also prone to commit crimes. WISE SAYINGS FOR BOYS AND GIRLS provides opportunities for things to think and talk about. Each of the sayings in the book can start a discussion since it is likely to excite the curiosity of the young ones. Since it is said that a proverb is not a proverb until you find your life illustrating it, adults are likely to explain each of the sayings from experience. Differential age permits an adult parent to have lots of experiences from which his or her children can and do benefit. But, some children seem to be in a hurry to grow up; so they sometimes resent advice from their parents.

In the past the nuclear family, with the assistance of grandparents, raised children. Today, in the United States of America, one family in four is headed by a single parent, generally a woman. If the single parent works outside the home, then the task of raising her child is further complicated by the fact that she has less energy available to her for raising her child or children. In that situation, the child either raises himself or herself on the neighborhood streets. One of the questions to consider is: How can one person do the work of two effectively when there is no change in the time available to do the work? Isn't it elementary knowledge that quality of performance is positively related to available resources for child-raising? In other words, the more the resources (in this case, the number of people, parents or guardians) the greater is the likelihood of success in child-raising.

There is no doubt that parents love their children very dearly, but the fact remains that a person cannot give what he or she does not possess. Each person has a limited amount of energy to devote to raising a child on a daily basis. If that energy is depleted in any way in the routine of life, less energy consequently remains to be devoted to raising the child. Child-

Preface

rearing is a full-time job. Child-raising becomes a drudgery when kids are rebellious, rude, and uncooperative. *WISE SAYINGS* can surely help. Given the fact that many other factors compete for time and energy, a mother does whatever is do-able to raise her child. Remember that millions of parents and children fall in to this category, and are doing an excellent job today. Remember, also, that one of the sayings in the book says that the largest room in the world is the room for improvement. Humans can always do more at any given time. The point I am making is that *WISE SAYINGS* is not meant as a criticism of current parental child-raising practices. In other words, it is not predicated on a deficit model. *WISE SAYINGS* is not just designed to make kids think deeply in everyday situations, but to encourage them to follow thoughts with actions that are carefully planned out. Kids love action, but action without thought is foolish-just as thought without action is empty.

Kids love company; they tend to be gregarious. They also tend to remember effortlessly information shared effectively with them by significant others. For these reasons, *WISE SAYINGS* can affect a child in a whisper even when there is no one around to look over the shoulders of the child. At work and play, in private and public places, kids have to behave the way their parents taught them or the way society expects them to behave. Society is based on a set of expectations.

Society is in the life of everyone of us: it is in our thoughts, words and actions. Society has a set of expectations about all the individuals within her. Parents have a reason to expect the best for their kids. For that reason, parents spend a greater part of their lives raising their kids, teaching them by words and examples. *WISE SAYINGS* is an extension of teaching by words: they provide OTHER voices rather than noises. Kids need other voices in order to grow up harmoniously. Other voices—the voices of the dead and those of the living— are always available to those who care to find them. The place of other voices can be taken by noises—noises that clutter the environment and rob the growing child of a chance to drink from society's fountain of pure water. WISE SAYINGS can only help; it is not likely to hurt a kid. Adults are required to speak the "word" in the presence of kids, and leave its secret growth to the universe. But, adults should be careful lest their personal behavior contradict their words.

To summarize, many children and young people do not hear the type of voices they could (not should) hear at the right time, at the impressionable age. Some parents, teachers and counselors have a hard time communicating effectively with children and young people. Some young people have been known to walk out on their parents, slam the door shut, go into their rooms and just sulk. From this type of experience, some parents decide not to administer a 'medicine' that has a great potential for making their children better, healthier, and much more successful. The fact of the matter is that some children are not receptive to suggestions, advice, etc.

WISE SAYINGS is likely to appeal to children and young people because it provides a chance for them to discover what is considered moral science and wisdom. At least, the introduction of a wise saying is likely to make a young person alert and be more attentive. Consider, for example, the saying "Twenty children cannot play together for twenty years." Isn't that likely to make a young person ask for an elaboration? In the process of explaining why it might be impossible for 20 children to be able to play together for twenty years, the parent, teacher or counselor has an excellent opportunity to share information.

Preface

I believe that children and young people should be made strong from within, and that they should be 'caught' young. One can bend a young twig; a grown tree is hard to bend. WISE SAYINGS gives parents, teachers, counselors, etc. another form of access to reach the mind of the child and the student.

HIGHLIGHTS

WISE SAYINGS is very unique in that it seeks to challenge our thinking faculties no matter where we are, whether it be at work or play. There is the belief that children have the capacity to absorb that which is impressed on their young mind: that is probably why children learn new and foreign languages faster and much more easily than adults.

Highlights of WISE SAYINGS are:

1. A reliance upon a variety of words of wisdom from different cultural backgrounds.

2. A selection of words of wisdom that seem to meet the needs of children, young people, and even adults. Since no one knows everything, we all need to learn.

3. A selection that is quotable and amenable to discussion. Most of the sayings are quotes that some adults can learn from if they themselves have never heard them or experienced them in any way before. If an adult has heard a particular saying before, familiarity with that saying is not likely, I believe, to lead to contempt.

Finally, the whole text is categorized as follows:

(I) Advice

(II) Philosophy

(III) Thought-Provoking

(IV) Other

The reader will discover at once where the emphasis lies from the categories identified above. It soon becomes clear that a greater portion of the text falls under the category of 'thought-provoking.'

It appears that these four categories or sections are self-explanatory. The distinction between categories (II) and (III) is very fine. I make no apologies for that decision. In the last category, one will find materials of an economic, political and/or historical interest.

It is not our intention that materials in one section be covered before going to the next one. The teacher, parent, counselor, student or whoever is acting as facilitator for a fruitful discussion is free to choose which materials he or she is going to use for maximum results.

An additional intent of WISE SAYINGS is to get young people to learn to think so they can see the beauty of our small world. Right now, it does not appear that the educational system in this country teaches young people to think deeply and effectively. WISE SAYINGS provides something to think about, talk about or argue about. The more they talk about it, the more they are likely to know about the particular topic. In short, WISE SAYINGS is both mental and spiritual

Preface

nutrition for students, parents, teachers, counselors, etc. There are enough materials to fill and entertain a vacant hour, thereby shutting out boredom. There is something for everyday of the year!

WISE SAYINGS is amply illustrated to give it an added interest. The book is designed so that it can be carried in coat pockets or in a satchel. It should be a constant companion to all who love wisdom and believe in social change through social learning and conditioning. Don't tell me kids hate to read: many of them hate to read what they consider lies!

HOW TO USE "WISE SAYINGS"

The material in WISE SAYINGS divides into four sections as explained above. The book does not follow any order other than an alphabetical one. In order to achieve maximum success, users of the book are encouraged to follow these suggestions:

1. Take one saying per week and focus on it whenever you have a chance to share with the child(ren) or students. Answer all questions asked by your child, ward or students as honestly as you can. Be willing to acknowledge your own limitation by saying 'I don't know' whenever it applies.

Use remarks such as 'I think...' 'In my opinion...' 'It seems to me...' in your attempts to explain whatever you are trying to get across to your child(ren), ward or students. Educated people tend to make probability statements in communication.

2. Encourage the child(ren) or students to illustrate the saying you are dealing with. The illustration could take various forms. Debates can be organized around a particular

saying. Let the children (students) have fun with WISE SAYINGS. Besides, let students work out the exercises suggested in *THE WISE SAYINGS MANUAL*.

3. A child who can read should be encouraged to study as many sayings as he or she wishes to study. Students can be encouraged to make their own collection.

4. Students can research the environments of certain sayings—people, places and things. Some information about people, places and some things included in certain sayings is provided at the end of the book. Students should be encouraged to do further research in that area and further inform themselves.

To ensure that children and students understand each saying chosen for study, a clear statement should be requested of each of them. Most of the steps required for effective study are indicated in *THE WISE SAYINGS MANUAL*.

First, ask the child what the saying means to him or her in words or other gestures. A saying that is well learned should be used. Happily, children and students are, generally speaking, good at using new things.

EVALUATION

One way to find out how effective WISE SAYINGS is is to evaluate the attitude of your child(ren) or students about six weeks after introduction of the contents of the book to the child(ren) or students. Some of the questions to ask for purposes of evaluation are:

1. Is my child (student) more attentive and logical than before?

_____ *Preface*

2. Is my child (student) more observant than before?

3. Is my child (student) more intellectually active than before?

By Junior High, a child should be able to read *WISE SAYINGS* effectively, and be in a position to talk about a wide range of topics, topics covered in the book and related topics not specifically dealt with. Young people would like to read what appeals to them; doing that might make them uncover more of the treasures of the ages. Students in Junior High should tackle the exercises in *THE WISE SAYINGS MANUAL*.

Parents, teachers and counselors would advance the cause of learning if they would write to the publishers, indicating what they like or do not like about *WISE SAYINGS*. Mature students and adults can also write to the publishers.

Adebisi T'Olu. Aromolaran
Oakland, California 1992

Section 1
ADVICE

ADVICE

To begin with, it appears that age and experience play a significant part in the lives of individuals everywhere. In primary groups, especially in families, the age differential factor affects child-raising practices and outcomes. Consider a child who is born into a family where the parents are each 20 and another child who is born into a family where the mother is 31 and the father, 38. The age and experience of the adults in the two cases is likely to affect quite significantly how each family raises their child.

Advice is a type of resource that makes life worth living. For that reason, it is important to define the term before we go any farther. According to the Webster New Collegiate Dictionary, the word "Advice" is defined, among others as, "recommendation regarding a decision or course of conduct: counsel; information or notice given; an official notice concerning a business transaction," for example a remittance advice.

Advice can be personal or directed to a group or a company. A parent must, of necessity, give advice to his or her child(ren). A teacher, preacher, or counselor may give advice to a person or a group of persons. In each of these situations, the age or experience differential factor matters. Coupled with that is the training of the facilitator. Teachers, preachers, counselors are generally well-trained. I am not too sure who trains parents-to-be or what type of training prospective parents undergo. Is there any need for prospective parents to get a measure of training?

There is another type of advice that does not depend upon age or experience differential. Legal advice or other forms of technical advice is not a factor of age or experience. For

Wise Sayings for Boys and Girls

example, a 60-year-old person may seek legal advice from an attorney who is 20 years younger than he or she. Advice is very important, but young people generally think that adults do not allow them to do their own thing.

Surely, adults want to share wisdom and experience with younger people. A mother wants her daughter or her son to shine on the stage of life; she gives some advice about friendship and friends, about hard work and savings, dating and marriage, house chores and helping habits, etc. Study after study has shown how rebellious young people are in the United States of America. There are even cases where young people are not only abusive to their parents but have also been known to be violent just because mother said daughter could not go on a date or that the young man of her affection was not up to par. I believe young people are likely to change once the scales fall off their eyes, and they realize that advice generally helps.

It is still a mystery why some young people sometimes reject the advice of their parents, but are eager to consider that same advice when it comes from a peer. Does the saying hold true for young persons that familiarity breeds contempt? Some teachers are sometimes more credible than a parent in the eyes of some children.

I do hope that young persons would pay particular attention to this section of the book before going to the other sections. I hope young people would keep an open mind, and value the advice given them by parents, teachers, preachers, counselors, etc. Instead of rejecting advice outright, young people should think about a piece of advice critically and decide whether or not it is good for them. I wish good sense would prevail.

Advice

There is some advice I have for all my readers: it is **this**, that young people ensure that a discussion of these sayings within groups - primary or secondary - would not result in blows. A good point to remember is that words are generally incapable of painting an accurate picture. You probably remember the saying: A picture is worth a thousand words.

I encourage my readers - particularly parents, teachers, and counselors - to train young people in the art of effective thinking. In particular, young people need to be encouraged to make statements in terms of probabilities, thereby avoiding making statements that are neither too wide nor too narrow. Young people should learn that a person's point of view is very important and should be respected.

Wise Sayings for Boys and Girls

1. A chicken kept in a run to keep it from danger complains that it is not allowed to go to the dunghill to play.

2. A dog keeps quiet in the presence of a lion.

3. A fierce dog generally does not watch two different households at the same time.

4. A promise is a debt; once you make it, you must pay that debt or else very few people will trust you.

5. A spendthrift does not realize that what is plentiful will become exhausted.

6. A word is enough for the wise; it is for him or her to fill up the gap.

7. Aim high;
   Aim at the sun,
   That way, you may reach the moon.

8. An elephant's head is not a fitting load for a child.

9. Are you paying too much for a particular commodity? Shop around to beat the high price!

10. Be a star, but let your light brighten other lives.

11. Be not wise in your own eyes.

12. Being at the wrong place, the wrong time can be very costly.

13. Believe not those who say the upward path is smooth.

_____ *Advice*

14. Better be late than the late.

15. Beware of fair weather friends.

16. Brevity is the soul of wit.

17. Children, you're very little,
    And your bones are very brittle;
    If you would grow great and stately,
    You must learn to work sedately.

18. Choose your friends with the same care you choose your underwear.

19. Cleanliness is next to Godliness.

20. Cut your coat according to your size.

21. Do not be led by the nose.

22. Do not count your chickens before they are hatched.

23. Do not forget your God or your home wherever you chance to wander; keep yourself from quarrelling, beware of people that are the snare of youth, and set a watch upon your tongue, which is not of the best.

24. Do not trouble trouble lest trouble troubles you.

25. Do you become an adult the day you turn 18?

26. Do you cut your nose to spite your face?

27. Don't be disappointed: turn every disappointment into an appointment.

28. Don't look for a pin in a hay stack.

29. Don't wait for the day of battle before getting your weapons ready.

30. Find a shoulder to stand on, and you'll reach the stars.

31. First things first: nature obeys its own laws. Learn to crawl before you walk.

32. For lack of a vision, the people perish.

33. Gaining physical growth without wisdom leads to disaster.

34. Get to the point instead of beating about the bush.

35. Give everyone your ear, but very few your tongue.

36. Give me one word that best describes life: Experience.

37. Give me some food, some clothing and shelter, but don't deny me an opportunity to grow spiritually and intellectually.

38. Go to the ants, thou sluggard.

39. Grow up by discovering something new about yourself everyday.

40. Have goodness in your heart; let people see it in your face; let it flow through your hands.

41. Hear your father's instruction, and reject not your mother's teaching.

Advice

Hear your father's instruction, and reject not your mother's teaching.

42. Honor and shame from no condition rise;
    Act well your part; there all the honor lies.

43. If at first you don't succeed, try, try, try again.

44. If no party meets your ideals, start you own; it's not fun to be politically homeless.

45. If trouble is sleeping by the side of the road, don't wake him up.

46. If you fail in the day of adversity, your strength is small.

47. If you plan to move up in life, think about three things above all others: task, time, technology- the 3 T's - and you're close to the wisdom of the ages.

48. If you throw a stone into the marketplace, you may hit a person from your own household.

49. If you're fit to live with a person, you should be fit to talk to him or her.

50. It is no use being angry with the head and putting the hat on the buttocks.

51. Keep a gold locket in your right hand; a diamond locket in the left; unless the hands are open, they do no one any good.

52. Leadership emerges everyday in young people: listen to their voice; watch their deeds.

53. Learn to stand up for the truth as you know it; seek to

Advice

improve that which you think you know; for knowledge can keep just as long as fish.

54. Learn useful things in the morning of life; work hard during the day, rest in the evening.

55. Let your hands minister to your necessities.

56. Let's not cry over spilt milk.

57. Life is a game: learn the rules, play the game.

58. Light and darkness don't belong together: do not choose a crooked person for a friend.

59. Like all good things you have, you have to earn a good name.

60. Listen to advice and accept instruction that you may gain wisdom for the future.

61. Look before you leap: things are not as they seem.

62. Make a habit of putting something by for the future: you'll never lack any good thing.

63. Make haste slowly.

64. Make a habit of transforming yourself by nourishing your spirituality. If you feed your spirituality, you'll be continuously renewed.

65. Mind your own business; people should attend to their own affairs.

Wise Sayings for Boys and Girls

66. Neither a borrower nor a lender be.

67. No plan is complete without an alternative. For every plan you make, have an alternative plan.

68. Obedience is better than sacrifice.

69. One assumes you love life and that you're determined to preserve life—your life and that of others.

70. One does not protect another person's head at the expense of allowing one's head to be carried away by a hawk.

71. One should not go to bed with the roof on fire.

72. One should not have too many irons in the fire.

73. One should not parade one's good fortunes to the public.

74. People, places and things are interrelated; become a leader of thought, and your stature becomes recognizable everywhere.

75. Put anger away lest it puts you out.

76. Put something by for a rainy day.

77. Put your own product out in a market economy, and watch your status grow.

78. Say 'yes', but have the courage to say 'no' whenever necessary. Avoid saying Yes/No, No/Yes.

79. Show hospitality intelligently: you may be entertaining some angels.

Advice

80. Show me your friends and I'll tell you the company you keep.

81. Shut the door on cant; open your mind to wisdom and action.

82. Since most of your actions have an effect, doesn't it behoove you to stop and count the cost of your intended action? To be wise after the event could cost you a lot.

83. Since you're not an island, and, no one really is, it behooves you to build up trust so that your efforts may have a greater chance of success.

84. Smile, no matter what; that way, you warm up the world with love.

85. Step into the future confidently: you're an eagle not a chicken.

86. Strike while the iron is hot.

87. Take away the beam in your own eyes, then you'll be able to see the speck in your brother's eyes.

88. Take care of the pennies, and the dollars will take care of themselves.

89. Take what you're given, and continue to ask for more.

90. Talk less, but think more: that way you have a lot more to offer in the long run.

91. Talk to me about time and money: the former I have; the latter, I want to know how to make.

92. Tell it to yourself that your fist will never have a human victim; that you will control your thoughts and tongue so they hurt no one; that you'll defend with all your resources everything and everyone who needs defending.

93. The busy bee has a reason for working; how about you?

94. The secret door to success is wide open, but you have to have the eyes to see it.

95. The stars keep their track and shine. Do you notice that constancy in nature?

96. There's a gap in 'Think and Grow Rich': fill that gap with positive action-plans.

97. There's a time to work;
There's a time to play;
Only foolish people play all the time.

98. There's really no break in learning: successful people go on learning in the school of life.

99. Think not that life is a bed of roses.

100. Think of the bee-hive and the sweetness of cooperation.

101. Those who live in a glasshouse should never throw stones.

102. Thoughts travel faster than sound: get them to work for you.

103. Three things, among others, ought to claim your attention: time, task and technology.

Advice

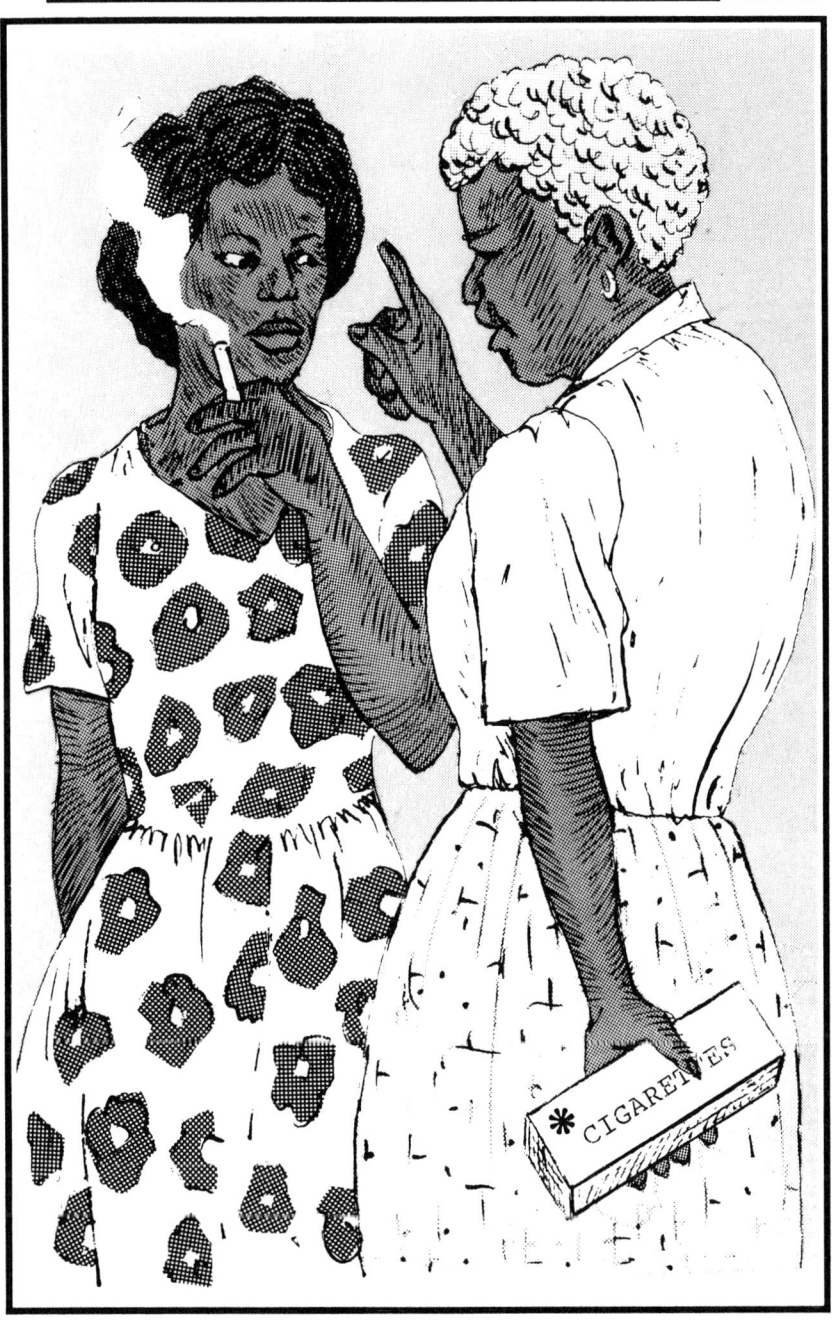

Those who live in a glass house should never throw stones.

104. "Tick-tock" says the clock.
Time is flying swift away;
"Tick-tock" says the clock,
Moments gone do not return.

105. Time is money; plan your daily 24 hours efficiently.

106. To succeed in today's world, you're going to need more than the five senses; you have to develop the sixth sense so you can be one step ahead of those who wish to pull you down.

107. To thine own self be true,
And it follows as the night the day,
You cannot be false to other people.

108. Touch someone today, but let it be a touch of love, the way you would want somebody to touch you.

109. Want not, waste not.

110. When a child acts like a child, an adult should act like an adult.

111. When you cut a tree in the forest, imagine what your reaction will be if such an act is done to you.

112. When you have some task to perform, first think about the formula: $SA.HE=T^2$, where SA means Spiritual Awareness; HE stands for Human Efforts; T^2 stands for Super Triumph.

113. Wherever you go; wherever you are, do not say 'yes' when you mean to say 'no'.

_____ *Advice*

114. Why wait for a pound of flesh which you cannot get? Forgive and forget: so you can move on.

115. Wish yourself well; wish other people well; that which you put out comes back to you.

116. Words and deeds that raise others' eyebrows hardly become a good person.

117. Work now when you can so that you may not wish to work when you cannot.

118. Work on yourself effectively: there'll be one less grumbler in the world.

119. Work while you work;
Play while you play.
To be useful and happy—
This is the way.

120. Yell when you can, but hold not anger in your veins.

121. Yield to other users of traffic, but never yield to temptation.

122. You cannot have your cake and eat it.

123. Your name is your identity: keep it where nothing can spoil it.

SECTION 2
PHILOSOPHY

PHILOSOPHY

This section has been termed 'Philosophy'. I owe it to you to say what that term means and why I have chosen that term. Do not be frightened by that term; do not think the term belongs to the college people or people of that group.

What does 'philosophy' mean? A dictionary definition has this to say: "pursuit of wisdom; a search for a general understanding of values and reality by chiefly speculative rather than observational means; an analysis of the grounds of and concepts expressing fundamental beliefs."

I have chosen the definitions stated above because those are the ones that are most relevant to this book.

I sincerely believe that young people have a need to seek and pursue wisdom, which is the art of thinking right and doing things right, although you may say that what is considered right depends on who is doing the defining. It is agreed that no one can define a situation for another person, but there is a general agreement about certain things which appear to be axioms. A few mathematical axioms are probably in place here:

    (i) Equals added to equals, the results are equal.
    (ii) Equals taken away from equals, the results are equal.
    (iii) Equals divided by equals, the results are equal.
    (iv) Equals multiplied by equals, the results are equal.

Each one of the statements above is an axiom: each one is self-evident, and requires little or no proof.

This section of the book provides several examples of what

the author considers philosophical (the general approach toward philosophy). Consider, for example, the saying: "Unity is strength." Apparently, this is a metaphor. Two things which differ in kind - unity, strength - are equated in a particular respect. It appears that the truth in that statement is self-evident.

Does "Evil communications corrupt good manners" ring a bell for you? In this case, the world has probably witnessed many occasions where evil communications have corrupted good manners.

Every one of us has the ability to think; every one of us can use resources that can do us some good. Philosophy tends to sharpen our thinking, it tends to challenge each one of us, young or old; it is a very powerful tool. Young people tend to love power, but they probably do not know that one of the greatest powers available to humans is mental power. It is possible for you to think yourself into anything you choose – life, health, wealth, creativity, etc.

Philosophy is not an end in itself: it is a means to an end. It is not enough to know the definition of a hand; it is equally important to use one's hands to supply one's needs wherever and whenever possible.

Philosophy first became popular in Africa several thousand years ago. Some young Greek students came over to Africa to study the new branch of knowledge, among them, Aristotle, Plato, Socrates, Alexander the Great, etc. It is probably true that philosophy changed substantially the lives of the Greek people. Socrates did teach young people to pursue knowledge relentlessly. Socrates' method of asking a series of questions soon made enemies for him among his people.

Philosophy

There are a great many philosophers who lived within the last two centuries; among these are Mahatma Ghandi, Martin Luther King, Jr., Elijah Muhammad, Marcus Garvey, Malcolm X, Kwame Nkrumah, W.E.B. DuBois, Obafemi Awolowo, Nnamdi Azikiwe, Julius Nyerere, etc. Of these, Martin Luther King, Jr., Kwame Nkrumah, W.E.B. Dubois, and Nnamdi Azikiwe studied philosophy formally, that is, they studied it in college.

No one is likely to persecute you for thinking your own thoughts in this day and age. By all means, learn to pursue wisdom: you have nothing to lose but your ignorance.

Logic - the art of reasoning - has always formed a needful part of philosophy. In ancient times, logic formed a part of the curriculum in Kemet's elementary schools. ("Kemet" is assumed to be the original name of the area now known as 'Egypt'. The terms 'Egypt' and 'Ghana,' among others, are Arabic.) Effective thinking can affect your life in very many ways.

Wise Sayings for Boys and Girls

124. A bird in the hand is worth two in the bush.

125. A chain is as strong as its weakest link.

126. A child's hand cannot reach the high shelves nor can an adult's enter into the gourd.

127. A crooked firewood dislocates the hearth; a wicked person disturbs the home.

128. A crushing burden is no adornment.

129. A friend in need is a friend indeed.

130. A mind is a terrible thing to waste.

131. A tormentor makes his/her victims hardy.

132. Absence makes the heart grow fonder.

133. Butterflies compare themselves with birds but cannot act like birds.

134. By wisdom a house is built, and by understanding it is established.

135. Charity begins at home.

136. Children are an inheritance of the earth.

137. Curiosity kills the cat.

138. Disobedience is the father of disrespect.

139. Empty barrels make the most sound.

Philosophy

Butterflies compare themselves with birds but cannot act like birds.

Wise Sayings for Boys and Girls

140. Every disappointment is a blessing in disguise.

141. Evil communications corrupt good manners.

142. Fools rush in where angels fear to tread.

143. He laughs best who laughs last.

144. He who commits adultery with another person's wife has no good intention toward that person.

145. Health is wealth.

146. Hope springs eternal in the human breast.

147. In a free economy, the consumer is king.

148. Knowledge is power; ignorance, despair.

149. Lack of planning leaves a big hole in your life.

150. Logic is one of the most powerful tools in the hands of an oppressor; without it the oppressor has no one to oppress.

151. Make new friends, but keep the old;
One is silver, but the other's gold.

152. Mother is gold; father is the looking glass.

153. Necessity is the mother of invention.

154. One person's meal is another person's poison.

155. Only by the spirit shall the nations be great.

156. Opportunity knocks but once.

Philosophy

157. Our one concern is that our stupid child shall not die, but what greater cause of death is there than stupidity?

158. Preparation is half the battle.

159. Pride goes before a fall.

160. Respect takes nought off, but adds more.

161. Rest is sweet after labor.

162. Seeing is believing.

163. Self-reverence, self-knowledge, self-respect; These three alone lead life to sovereign power.

164. Slow and steady wins the race.

165. Some failures are sometimes more successful than success.

166. Still waters run deep.

167. Stone walls do not a prison make nor iron bars a gate.

168. Ten sparrows do not make a summer.

169. The child is father of the man.

170. The evil that people do lives after them; the good is often buried with their bones.

171. The mice will play when the cat's away.

172. The patient person who has learned to wait finds that only ripe apples fall to his or her waiting hands.

Wise Sayings for Boys and Girls

The world is a stage.

_____ *Philosophy*

173. The world is a stage.

174. The world is like a turbulent sea, the inhabitants are like a collection of water; since all waters flow to the sea only those who know how to swim in it can enjoy life.

175. They also serve who only stand and wait.

176. Those born to be leaders are few; those born to serve them are many.

177. Those who have strong hands, but would not work with them truly mark themselves out for poverty.

178. Time is the healer of all wounds.

179. To err is human; to forgive, divine.

180. Too many cooks spoil the broth.

181. Uneasy lies the head that wears the crown.

182. Unequal combinations are always disadvantageous to the weaker side.

183. Unity is strength.

184. Wealth brings many new friends, but a poor person is soon deserted by friends.

185. When the impatient person shakes the apple tree, both ripe and unripe apples fall down.

186. Where there's a will, there's a way.

187. Wisdom is better than jewels.

188. Wisdom is justified by her deeds.

189. Work is the cure for poverty.

190. Working leads to self-discovery.

191. You're a small universe within a larger one.

192. You're the salt of the earth.

Section 3
THOUGHT-PROVOKING

THOUGHT-PROVOKING

In this section is collected sayings that are likely to fall within the experience of many readers, young and old. The topics covered in this section range from little things to big ones.

Consider, for example, the two couplets cited below, both being from Alexander Pope:
> A little learning is a dang'rous thing
> Drink deep or taste ne'er the Pierian spring;
> There, shallow draughts intoxicate the brain,
> And drinking largely sobers us again.

This extract is likely to appeal to young people and push them in the direction of action. Surely, young people do not like to be described as ignorant. The fact that the young people themselves make this discovery is likely to make them want to pursue knowledge.

Thought is critical in the lives of all humans, but particularly in the lives of young people. It is known that many young people do thoughtless things such as lying, playing hookie, drinking and driving, wanting to walk before crawling, etc.

It has been said that children between the ages of 3 and 7 ask endless questions of their parents or guardians. It appears that children learn a great deal from questioning adults about the things that are dark to them. This section of the book is designed to make adults, too, ask questions of young people. There is probably no justification at all to brutalize a child for saying or behaving in a certain way. One of the ways to teach a child effectively is probably through questioning. It appears only logical: young people ask questions of adults and learn from them; adults may learn to use the Socratic method effectively. Some trials may convince them.

It pays to think deeply, but the art of thinking has to be taught to young people. Mother has to teach the children to think; father has to pitch in and encourage his sons to think. The child's mind must be cultivated: an uncultivated mind is a wasted mind.

Who is to cultivate the mind of the young people of this land? Can we cultivate our young people with tired hands and minds? These are some of the questions that we seek to answer by putting across to all our young people WISE SAYINGS FOR BOYS AND GIRLS. It does not appear that one can provoke thought in any other way other than by encouraging young people to get involved in the art of thinking at a very early age.

Of course, most human environments are full of thought-provoking things, people, animals, birds, insects, plants, etc. Parents and teachers are reminded that young people are likely to be better off if they learn to make observations early in life.

To assume that every child in the United States of America has access to adults who hover around it 24 hours a day, teaching it how to make observations is probably false. The fact of the matter is that many homes have just a single parent, generally a woman.

The problem is not with the sex of the head of the family, but rather with the number of people in a kinship relationship with the growing child. The female or the male head is just one person: one is not a substitute for the other. Parents have enough problems raising their kids, but parental authority seemed to have come to their aid in very difficult situations. Step-parents or acquaintances trying to assist in raising their spouse's or friend's children sometimes have a harder time.

Thought Provoking

Children are sticklers: they sometimes desire to bond with an absent parent, no matter how green the grass is around them.

Strong logic, as opposed to a weak logic, is probably learned rather than inherited. In many African societies, the extended family, rather than the nuclear, forms the structure, the physical and nonphysical environments within which the child operates interactively. In that way, kinship members share frankly with one another, and go through life in a spirit of adventure, each one relying upon the strong support services provided by the group.

The sayings categorized as Thought-Provoking are likely to be easily digestible to parents, teachers and counselors. I emphasize that the sayings must be digestible to adults who would then be in an advantageous position to share them with their children, students or clients.

To assist users of *WISE SAYINGS* to do an excellent job, the publishers decided to provide a manual: **THE WISE SAYINGS MANUAL**. This should be available in book stores across the country. Users of *WISE SAYINGS* would then discover the joy of working with children.

193. A child grows into an adult, but does the child know that only men of quality respect women's equality?

194. A child trying to act like an adult will find that his or her age is an obstacle.

195. A gentleman never inflicts pain.

196. A healthy body is the guest-chamber of the soul; a sick one, its prison.

197. A journey of a thousand miles begins with a single step.

198. A little learning is a dangerous thing;
Drink deep or taste ne'er the Pierian spring.
There, shallow draughts intoxicate the brain,
And drinking largely sobers us again.

199. A person who fights and runs away will live to fight another day.

200. A person who relies only on the promises of inheritance is on the sure road to penury.

201. A quarrel which arises from envy dies hard.

202. A rolling stone gathers no moss.

203. A smoker is a foolish person on the one end and fire on the other.

204. A soft answer turns away wrath.

205. A stitch in time saves nine.

Thought Provoking

206. A tamed mind is likely to find more fun in life than an untamed one.

207. A thing of beauty is a joy forever.

208. A troublesome person does not allow a quiet person to remain quiet.

209. A wise person is mightier than a strong person.

210. A wise person never eats with ten fingers.

211. A young person who knows how to wash his/her hands will dine with the elders.

212. Action without thought is foolish; thought without action is empty.

213. All that glitters is not gold.

214. Ambition's gate has never let in a well-contented guest.

215. An elder who goes to excess loses respect in the group.

216. An ounce of help is worth more than a pound of pity.

217. Anything that is worth doing requires an effort.

218. As you make your bed, so you must lie in it.

219. Bad news travels fast.

220. Bats do not fly until it is dusk.

221. Beauties in vain their pretty eyes may roll;
Charms strike the sight, but merit wins the soul.

Wise Sayings for Boys and Girls

222. Birds of the same feathers flock together.

223. Blaming others tends to blind you to your own faults.

224. Blood is thicker than water.

225. Both education and occupation positively affect social class. Education provides the energies with which one climbs the social ladder.

226. By helping others, you help yourself.

227. By suffering comes wisdom.

228. By your thoughts you're blessed; by your thoughts you're sorely hurt.

229. Can the blind guide the blind?

230. Children rule City States only in a state of make-believe.

231. Confidence breeds confidence, and doubt, doubt.

232. Confusion grows in a community without leadership; a home becomes desolate for lack of a head.

233. Cowards die many times before their death;
The valiant never taste of death but once.

234. Death and life are in the power of the tongue.

235. Do you play at work and work at play?

236. Do you put things over persons in your choice of what is important to a successful life?

Thought Provoking

237. Even though work is available everywhere, finding it is awfully hard for some people.

238. Everybody's business is nobody's business.

239. Evil to those who evil think.

240. Exchange is no robbery: the world thrives on an exchange of goods and services.

241. Experience is the best teacher, particularly for fools.

242. Fair tresses man's imperial race ensnare,
And beauty draws us with a single hair.

243. Faith and fear are never friends: one betrays the other.

244. Familiarity breeds contempt.

245. For lack of knowledge, a people perish.

246. Good character is the adornment of humanity as white teeth are the adornment of a smile.

247. Good habits tend to preserve life; bad ones tend to snuff off life fast.

248. Gratitude is a debt a good student owes a good teacher.

249. Health and strength are better than any gold, a robust body better than untold wealth.

250. Heaven helps those who help themselves.

251. House and wealth are inherited from parents but a prudent wife is from 'Olodumare' (God in Yoruba beliefs).

252. How can a man who has bent himself make others straight?

253. How can you call for information if you can't read? How can you keep up with the state of your world if you don't read? How can you receive messages from the millions of famous writers if you've not formed a habit of reading?

254. How vain are all these glories, all our pains,
Except good sense preserve what beauty gains.

255. I have never seen an honest person suffer nor their children beg their bread.

256. I need help; for the good that I would I do not do; the evil that I would not that I do.

257. I shall not rest from mental fight, nor shall my sword sleep in my hand.

258. Ideas separate people; ideas bring people together.

259. If the consumer is king in a market economy, have you ever thought what the producer might be?

260. If you and your child are on fire, you'll first put out your own.

261. If you can walk, you can dance; if you can talk, you can sing.

262. If you do not watch what you eat, you'll have to watch what you weigh.

Thought Provoking

If you do not watch what you eat, you'll have to watch what you weigh.

263. If you're not working on yourself, you should think again.

264. If your appetite for education is large, you're not likely to need a doctor.

265. In prosperity you cannot always tell a true friend, but in adversity you cannot mistake an enemy.

266. In the game of life, a win-win situation is more interesting than a zero-sum situation.

267. It's a mistake to preserve gold rather than your name, for, once a name is spoilt, nothing can restore it.

268. Jealousy and anger shorten your days; worry brings premature old age.

269. Just as you can cause a storm in a tea-cup, you can cause a hurricane within yourself by thinking ineffectively.

270. Knowledge and money are different; with sharing, the former increases while the other decreases.

271. Knowledge is like sea water, the more of it you drink, the thirstier you become.

272. Learning to resolve conflicts ensures you don't have to keep company with loneliness.

273. Learning to think is probably the first step in enlarging your freedom.

274. Living without skills is like having an automobile without parts.

Thought Provoking

275. Love is patient and kind; it is not jealous or boastful; it is not arrogant or rude.

276. Machiavelli left a mark in politics: achieve addition through division.

277. Many people are wiser after the event: they reject the advice of elders only to regret in the end.

278. Maturity in thought, words, and deeds marks the change from childhood to adulthood; adults who behave like children are described as childish.

279. Minds are like parachutes: they function best only when open.

280. Money is a bad master but a good servant.

281. Money lost can be regained; moments gone do not return.

282. More things are wrought by prayer than this world dreams of.

283. Morning tends to show the day as childhood shows adulthood.

284. Most normal people recognize shame, and try to avoid it.

285. Most of human behavior is learned: one learns to be nice, another learns to be nasty.

286. Nature obeys its own laws: whatever goes up must come down.

287. Needs are easier to define than wants and desires.

288. No one can be as sympathetic as a mother; whoever reasons with his/her father builds up confidence.

289. No person is an island: humans function best in groups.

290. Once bitten, twice shy.

291. One clear example of nature's lessons for humans is water seeking its own level.

292. One door closes, another one opens. It's useless to stand and stare at a closed door while other doors are already open to you.

293. One good lesson to learn in life is asking for help.

294. One person's work is simply another's leisure activity.

295. One star outshines another in brightness, but do the stars grumble and complain?

296. One way to understand the working of a cohesive human group is observe the spokes on a bicycle wheel in motion.

297. One who initiates an evil pretends as if he or she knows nothing about it, and so keeps aloof.

298. One who misdirects his or her energies, however industrious, is no better than a lazy person.

299. Only those who have experienced joy and sadness know the difference between the two.

300. Patience is bitter, but its fruit is sweet.

Thought Provoking

301. People in cooperation tend to produce more than those in isolation.

302. Pleasant thoughts sometimes bring sad thoughts to the mind.

303. Politics sometimes makes strange bedfellows.

304. Prevention is better than cure.

305. Punctuality is the soul of business.

306. Quitters are never winners.

307. Rats desert a sinking ship.

308. Repetition aids memory; a good habit is the prop for a successful life.

309. School is the place for work and play, friends and fun, help and hope.

310. School: that's my place as I ask for help in understanding this wide, wonderful, beautiful world.

311. Similarity in habits enables two persons to become friends.

312. Some books are meant to be tasted; others, to be read and digested.

313. Style of speech rather than content of speech rarely win elections.

314. Taking a decision alone makes one responsible for its consequences, but one person cannot be held respon-

sible for the decisions of many.

315. Taxes are as sure as death in a capitalistic economy.

316. The child who says 'I can' will climb to the hill top; The child who says 'I can't', will at the bottom stop.

317. The door that leads to success and happiness is narrow; the door that leads to misery is wide.

318. The fewer your teachers in life, the harder it becomes for you to gain access to a wide array of information.

319. The habits that one cultivates in childhood generally last a lifetime.

320. The largest room in the world is the room for improvement.

321. The law is an ass: anyone can ride it.

322. The love of money is the root of most evil.

323. The mouth does not say everything the eye sees.

324. The needle, though small, is not such as the chicken can swallow.

325. The pen is mightier than the sword.

326. The person who pays the piper dictates the tune.

327. The problem is not just voting, but voting intelligently.

328. The right hand washing the left keeps both hands clean.

_____*Thought Provoking*

329. The rulers and the ruled wield power at different times.

330. The safety of the tree is the safety of the bird (that perches on it).

331. The thief who steals the king's bugle: where is he going to blow it?

332. The way we think, talk and work generally prepares us for our social position in the community.

333. The wild cat does not roam about during the day; people of good breeding do not roam about at night.

334. The wisest fool is the person who saves money and wastes time.

335. The world is a marketplace: buyers and sellers are connected by price.

336. There are six things which God hates, seven which are clearly an abomination before the same God: haughty eyes, a lying tongue, and hands that shed innocent blood, a heart that devises wicked plans, feet that make haste to run to evil, a false witness who breathes out lies, and a man who sows discord among brothers.

337. There're markets everywhere: neighborhood, national and international markets. Where are your own products and services competing?

338. There're three skill areas you should know about; three that you should learn to use: life, group, and technical.

339. There's nothing good or bad: thinking makes it so.

Wise Sayings for Boys and Girls

*The wild-cat does not roam about during the day;
people of good breeding do not roam about at night.*

_____Thought Provoking

340. There's nothing like friends who never quarrel, and enemies who never reconcile.

341. Thinking of a wolf is enough to kill a dog.

342. Those who die as a result of their folly are many; those who die as a result of their wisdom are few.

343. Those who have no roots to claim tend to claim relation ship with other people.

344. Those who live by the sword shall die by the sword.

345. Thoughts have wings; they can and do fly.

346. Time wastes those who waste time.

347. To know a person outside is not as much as to know what that person is like at home.

348. Troubles never come singly.

349. Truth never strays, but lying wanders into the bush.

350. Twenty children cannot play together for twenty years.

351. Two rams cannot drink water from the same calabash.

352. Two wrongs never make a right.

353. Tyranny generally leads to democracy: the tree of liberty is watered by the blood of tyrants.

354. Uncontrolled desires and wants tend to swallow up one's income and other resources.
355. Unrequited love generally turns sour.

356. Untrained and intractable children generally learn their lessons through outsiders.

357. Voting gives you a voice in a democracy. Do people use their voices intelligently?

358. Wars spell destruction. Do people vote before declaring a war?

359. We can make our lives sublime: no one can do that by legislation.

360. We cannot survive unless we change; we will not change unless we survive.

361. We cease to live a happy life when we cease to communicate.

362. Wealth and poverty lie in your hands: you can make a choice as to which one to drop and which one to keep.

363. What affects the eye affects the nose.

364. What is worth doing at all is worth doing well.

365. What you fear most comes to you: you're a prisoner of your worst fears.

366. When elders are in the market, a child's head is not allowed to droop.

367. When mother dies, one loses a very precious stone; when father dies, one's looking glass disappears.

368. When people talk, they don't fight.

Thought Provoking

When elders are in the market, a child's head is not allowed to droop.

369. When you point an accusing finger at someone, you've pointed four to yourself.

370. Where's wisdom? What shall I give to gain it? I'll make any sacrifice to gain wisdom.

371. Wherever your treasure is there will your heart be also.

372. Whoever gives you an education gives you the greatest gift which no one can take away from you.

373. Whoever thinks a perfect thing to see,
Thinks what ne'er was nor is nor e'er shall be.

374. Work that turns you against yourself is not work: it's worse than slavery.

375. You shall reap whatsoever you sow:
High in the mountain,
Low in the valley,
You shall reap whatsoever you sow.

376. You won't understand democracy if you don't participate in it when you can.

377. Young people are the resources that go into the making of a strong nation.

378. Your ability to think is measured by what you do with your thoughts.

379. Your father and your mother probably told you different things about other people. Do you still hold onto that today without making your own observations?

SECTION 4
OTHER

OTHER

This is the fourth section of the book, but it is not the least. In this section will be found sayings dealing with time, work, play, income, sayings, law, labor, management, credit, demand, supply, price, choice, banking, wages, crime, Karl Marx, Ronald Reagan, Nelson Mandela, government, apartheid, etc.

Young people are growing persons who need to know more about their economic, political and other environments. Young people need to know about voting in a democratic system. It is possible that elections are held in schools for one office or another. If that were so, example is probably better than precepts. Consider for example the saying: "I believe in government; I have a voice, and must make that voice heard." Clearly, this is what participative democracy is all about. To get this across to children requires some ingenuity, but a practical situation can make it quite clear. The teacher could facilitate an election among all the students in a class.

One clear advantage for this section is that it can be enriched by the approaches used in the three previous sections. The art of thinking, the pursuit of wisdom, sharing wisdom - all these are not supposed to stop with the sections marked A,P, and T.

This section clearly presents opportunities to relate discussions to current human environments and activities such as work, play, price, etc. Some of the questions to consider are: What is work? What is play? What is a price? These elementary questions and their corresponding answers are very important in making or marring the growing child. For example: does the child see school as work? Why does one have to pay a price? Why can't one just go the the store and take what one wants? The answers to each of these questions are likely to set the stage for fruitful discussions.

Consider, for example a saying from the book, namely: "A teacher-student relationship exists everywhere: the world is a huge school." Here, for example is a great opportunity for everyone to make discoveries. To assist our process of discovery, let us consider another question so we can get back to the former. What makes a student-teacher relationship fruitful? I think, in this case, a useful answer is MUTUAL RESPECT, meaning the student respecting the teacher or the teacher symbol on the one hand, and the teacher respecting the student or the student symbol on the other.

I should like to draw attention to one more idea in this section just to whet the appetite of the user. The saying goes: "Communication is one thing: effective communication is quite another." This particular saying is likely to stir up a great deal of discussion, especially within a group. A wise facilitator - teacher, parent or counselor (I see each one as a facilitator of life) - can turn that saying into a project for the group. Ask the questions: What is effective communication? Do I communicate effectively? It can be fun if both parties are open-minded, so one group is able to learn by teaching, and the other group, teach by learning.

This section of the book is probably juicier than the other three. Given that situation, young people still require help; they still need to profit from the experiences of adults, the facilitators of their life.

I believe that if facilitators would give assignments to young people, then the young people would have something to think about, talk about, write about instead of standing

Other

around the corner from where they might be picked up for troubling trouble. Standing at the corner with friends to have a decent conversation can be fun up to a point. WISE SAYINGS can help young people see the light, and, probably find the way.

Wise Sayings for Boys and Girls

380. A bad credit arises not from your complexion or your size, but from agreed upon payments that were not made on time.

381. A bad worker tends to quarrel with his/her tools.

382. A crushing burden is no adornment.

383. A good education does not consist of just reading, writing and arithmetic, commonly called the 3 R's; it consists also of an education of the head, heart and hands, which I'll characterize as the 3 H's.

384. A lot of what you attempt to learn at school grew out of what other people have experienced in their lives.

385. A portion of what you put into the world comes to you personally; the rest is in store for your children.

386. A secret is hard to keep among three friends.

387. A single child is relatively difficult to raise. The parents generally have no alternative but to rely on what they think was the way they were raised.

388. A society without laws would not exist for long.

389. A teacher-student relationship exists everywhere: the world is a huge school.

390. Action speaks louder than voice.

391. Agreements and contracts: signing before reading them can and does cause you serious problems.

Other

392. An organization that does not recruit young people into its ranks will die a natural death.

393. Apartheid is a political fraud in which the minority rules the majority by all means necessary.

394. As you prepare young people to vote, so prepare them to rule.

395. Asking for credit is easy; paying for goods and services already received is not so easy.

396. By respecting my first teachers, my parents, it was easy for me to respect all my teachers in and out of school.

397. Cold war politics spread to areas that were neither cold nor hot.

398. Communication is one thing; effective communication is quite another.

399. Crossing the carpet is seen as a mark of personal conviction in politics.

400. Curiosity and discontent are related: they generally lead to discoveries.

401. Different people use their voting rights differently: some vote for a candidate on personal merits; others vote for the party that has the most attractive program for the people.

402. Do you negotiate a corner the same way you negotiate a business agreement?

WISE SAYINGS FOR BOYS AND GIRLS

Curiosity and discontent are related: they generally lead to discoveries.

_____ *Other*

403. Does the end justify the means?

404. Excess of joy makes the frog break its legs.

405. Experience is the best teacher, but can you experience everything?

406. Father talks about his political party; mother talks about her social club. As a child, what shall I talk about?

407. For everything there is a season, and a time for every matter under heaven:
a time to be born, and a time to die;
a time to plant and a time to pluck up what is planted;
a time to kill, and a time to heal;
a time to break down, and a time to build up;
a time to weep, and a time to laugh;
a time to mourn, and a time to dance;
a time to cast away stones, and a time to gather stones together;
a time to embrace, and a time to refrain from embracing;
a time to seek, and a time to lose;
a time to keep, and a time to cast away;
a time to rend, and a time to sew;
a time to keep silent, and a time to speak;
a time to love, and a time to hate;
a time for war, and a time for peace!

408. Freedom of thought and expression is inalienable: take it away and you have stopped progress itself.

409. Going afoul of the law can and does create roadblocks in your life's journey.

410. Groups reward their members; States define which acts

WISE SAYINGS FOR BOYS AND GIRLS

A time to plant and a time to pluck up what is planted

_____ *Other*

are criminal.

411. Haggling often adds fun to the exchange between the buyer and the seller.

412. Happy that we're not over happy.

413. Home-keeping youths have only homely wits.

414. Human beings are capable of negotiating anything: a breakdown in negotiations causes major problems.

415. Humans sometimes fly from what they know to what they know not: the grass is generally greener elsewhere.

416. Humans wait for time, time does not wait for anyone; rather, it moves on noiselessly.

417. I believe in governments; I have a voice, and must make that voice heard.

418. I don't go to school to be spoon-fed: my parents showed me going to school is my work.

419. I don't want to wait for my parents to tell me how important school is: I picked that idea up quick.

420. I learn to think at an early age: now, what appears hidden to others is quite clear to me.

421. I see my parents' correction of me as the manure that nourishes plants and makes them grow luxuriantly. Since I've accepted parental corrections, I've prospered.

422. I see with the eyes of the spirit: I see clearly the open way.

423. I vote for mutual respect, particularly in a learning environment.

424. If a blacksmith continues to strike a piece of iron at one same point, he or she must have a reason for doing so.

425. If environment is the nursery of life, how is life going to exist without a healthy environment?

426. If fire has no secret ally, it cannot cross a river.

427. If the consumer is king in a free economy, why is it that many more want to become producers and business owners?

428. If the people lead, the leaders will follow in earnest.

429. If there's a common ancestry for human-kind, does it make sense to discriminate against anyone on the basis of race?

430. If you beware of the law; the law would beware of you.

431. If you cannot read and write, your world is likely to be sadly limited.

432. If you don't know who you are, you can hardly appreciate other people.

433. If you give a person a fish, you feed that person for a day; if you teach that person to fish, you feed him or her for life.

434. If you see with the eyes of the spirit, you'll find tongues in trees, books in the running brook, and good in ev-

_____ *Other*

erything.

435. If you sell your labor to yourself, would you charge the same price as you charge other people?

436. If you study Nature, and yourself carefully, you'll make discoveries that are likely to create a balance in your life.

437. In the sweat of your face you shall eat bread.

438. Is politics learned? I wonder who the teachers are.

439. It is better to be poor and happy than to be rich and afraid.

440. It is one of two ways with a door: it opens either inward or outward; it shuts either inward or outward.

441. Life's ups-and-downs cannot be hidden: in families, they're indicated by periods of bloom and gloom respectively.

442. Little drops of water,
Little grains of sand,
Make the mighty oceans
And the lofty hills.

443. Living above one's means could be the cause of anxiety and other serious problems.

444. Love and hate are similar: the former warms up the body positively; the other simply overheats it.

445. Love zooms you to the stars; hate snuffs you to Hades.

446. Many kings have ruled their communities and States,

but King James I of England stands out: he's described as the wisest fool in Christendom.

447. Markets do one fantastic thing: they bring sellers and buyers together in a rewarding interaction.

448. Meanness shows in thoughts, looks, and deeds; a mean person hurts his or her mate in various ways.

449. Neither you nor your parents or guardians can afford everything you want or desire; they can, however, take care of most of your needs. Needs and desires are totally different from each other.

450. Nothing ensures the status quo like mental laziness; nothing changes it faster than thought and actions!

451. One cannot feed a lean child to become robust in just one day.

452. One thing leads to another either as cause or as consequence.

453. One who is called a hawk should not fail to seize a chicken.

454. Open hands and open minds keep resources in circulation, thus blessing the giver and the receiver.

455. Over-mighty children generally resent their parents' advice, but learn their lessons through harsh experiences.

456. Parents significantly affect their children's future roles: they make leaders or followers.

_____ *Other*

457. Peace has her victories, which if carefully examined, are no less renowned than war.

458. People are political animals: they band together for one thing or another.

459. People organize to bring about social change; oppressors organize to break up organized groups.

460. Political expression cannot take place without political education.

461. Politics is neither dirty nor negative; it's the actors and actresses in it who are either dirty or negative.

462. Protecting the physical environment should be a win-win rather than a win-lose situation.

463. Reagan and Marx are as poles apart as Mandela and Malan.

464. Sellers and buyers of labor have one thing in common: choice to sell or not to sell; to buy or not to buy: that is one of the choices people have to make.

465. Some people are born great; others achieve greatness; some have greatness thrust on them.

466. Some young people think that teachers are mean; they forget, however, that some teachers are sometimes cruel so as to be kind.

467. Supervision is an arm of organizations: governments supervise a State for progress.

468. The American Dream is sometimes one of the main

causes of the American dilemma.

469. The credit system allows the buyer to buy more conveniently and the seller to move more goods and services. When the buyer screws up, the seller applies the screw.

470. The Crimean War of 1853-1856 has been described as a crime.

471. The disease that afflicts the monkey does not afflict the vulture: the vulture is bald in his head, the monkey, at the buttocks.

472. The eye is the lamp of the body.

473. The face and the voice are an indication of the quality of a person's mind: these give you a strong clue to the person.

474. The glories of our blood and State,
Are shadows, not substantial things.

475. The more the number of wise voices around me, the happier I become. If I listen carefully to the voice of reason, I'll see clearly the obstacles on my way, and learn to move around those obstacles. I'm on the highroad to success.

476. The greatest divide in the working world is the change each one gets after taxes.

477. The hawk in the sky does not realize that those below are watching him.

478. The making of a pin teaches us a great lesson about ourselves: cooperation through division of labor saves

_____ *Other*

time and energy.

479. The more you work without resting, the less productive you become: fatigue sets in until you run out of energy.

480. The most exciting human experience is probably the pursuit of knowledge in a team spirit.

481. The tough keep going when the going gets tough.

482. There are three periods in the life of a human being: the morning, afternoon, and evening.

483. There're 4 M's you should be aware of as you grow up; these are: money, management, material, manpower. For the last, I should like to substitute 'labor' for manpower, but, I'd like to retain 4 M's.

484. There're those who want to teach; there are those who want to learn; interest brings these two groups together.

485. There're words and personalities that open doors; there are those that cause the door to be slammed in your face.

486. There're, among others, three types of questions: the one you ask others, those you ask yourself, and those others ask you.

487. There's a cost for most of the good things you enjoy in the world.

488. Those who succeed most in life harmonize themselves with nature.

489. Those who turn a deaf ear to the advice of their elders don't generally go far in life.

490. Three days to think about are yesterday, today, and tomorrow. The most important of these is today.

491. Time heals all wounds: we forgive others even when we don't forget the hurt.

492. We are all in the market together, someone wants to sell, someone wants to buy. It just depends on the product or the service, and the choices we make.

493. We learn to be prosperous just as we learn to be poor; one gradually drifts into success and failure.

494. What a shame! The poor have to pay more for everything.

495. What causes the earth to make way for the earthworm is one of the mysteries of Nature.

496. What is this life, if, full of cares
We have no time to stand and stare?

497. What works for me may not work for you: spiritual awareness opens most doors for me.

498. What's the main factor for the change in human habits? A change in the mode of thinking.

499. When a child makes money, he or she spends it, but when the child is in trouble, he or she brings the trouble home.

500. When a lazy man's sweetheart is old enough for marriage, a rich man would marry her.

501. When I was a child, I spoke like a child; I thought like a child; I reasoned like a child.

Other

502. When you tame yourself, and others tame themselves, our world becomes neater and livable.

503. Which part of the description of money impresses you most—scarce, valuable, divisible, easily recognizable?

504. Why give me milk if I cannot digest it nor Marx when I cannot understand it?

505. Wisdom is the key to a successful life, but it varies in individuals and that explains largely those who are happy and those who are not so happy.

506. Words are one thing; action is another.

507. You can take a person out of the country but you may not take the country out of him or her.

508. You pay a price for most of the things you have: that price is fixed by a combination of several factors, chief of which are demand and supply in a free economy.

509. You stand to gain a lot if you learn to make observations of people, places and things.

510. You stand upon a carpet of history—your family history, your ethnic history, your national and international history; that history is your guide.

511. You're a star, and can share the common characteristics of stars, namely, SHINE so as to brighten your part of the world.

512. Your logic gave you a job; your attitude can cost you that job.

513. Your success is my success, your joy is my joy, but your failure causes me pain.

514. Your word is a lamp to my feet.

DEFINITION OF TERMS NOTES ON REFERENCES

Apartheid means "set apart" or segregated. Apartheid was introduced into Azania around 1948 in an area that is still referred to as Southern Africa. Through apartheid laws, the Afrikaans, the minority group in southern Africa, have ruled the majority African ethnic groups since 1948.

Christendom is a term that refers to all the areas of the earth where the Christian doctrine is accepted, and where the then two Christian rulers of the Church—the Pope as the head of the Roman Catholics, and the King or Queen of England—reigned supreme, respectively. The term refers to the Christian world.

The Crimean War (1853 - 1856) The Crimean War started in 1853 when Turkey declared war on Russia. Russia had earlier occupied two provinces of Moldavia and Malachia. England and France joined Turkey in 1854, Sardinia in 1855. The saying was probably introduced because of the pun contained in 'Crimean' and 'crime'.

Alexander the Great (Alexander III, 356 - 323 B.C.). Alexander reigned as king of Macedon (336 - 323 B.C.) He was the son of Philip II. Alexander the Great was a warrior, but he was also interested in learning. He conquered most of the countries around the Mediterranean sea; he conquered Egypt. The city of Alexandria in north Africa is named after him.

Aristotle (384 - 322 B.C.) was a Greek philosopher, and a pupil of Plato, another Greek philosopher who had studied in Egypt, north-eastern Africa. Aristotle later became a tutor

Notes

to Alexander the Great. Aristotle was regarded as the founder of western scientific thought. If that statement holds true, then African teachers were probably the founders of western scientific thought.

Awolọwọ, Ọbafemi (1909-1987) Awolọwọ was born March 6, 1909 at Ikẹnnẹ, in Ijẹbu-Rẹmọ, western Nigeria. He was the son of a farmer. He attended mission schools and later worked as a newspaper reporter before becoming a trade union organizer. He studied privately and obtained a bachelor's degree in commerce. He later studied law in London where he wrote 'Path to Nigerian Freedom' in 1947. "Awo" as he is popularly called, founded a Yoruba cultural organization called 'Ẹgbẹ Ọmọ Oduduwa' which formed the stepping stone to the founding of the Action Group, a political organization. Awo became the first Premier of western Nigeria, and in 1960, became Leader of the Opposition in Nigeria's House of Representatives.

Azikiwe, Nnamdi (1904 -   ) Dr. Azikiwe was born at Zungeru, Northern Nigeria in 1904. Like most African leaders, he attended mission schools before leaving for the United States of America for higher education. Dr. Azikiwe was probably Africa's best-known journalist and nationalist. He fought British imperialism with all the resources at his disposal. He founded a string of newspapers, the best known of them being *'West African Pilot.'* He became Nigeria's first Head of State when Nigeria attained independence in 1960.

DuBois, W.E.B. (1868 - 1963), was one of the most important leaders of African American protest in the United States of America. He waged a relentless mental warfare against racism, discrimination, injustice, and oppression of minorities. In 1895 DuBois became the first African American to receive a PhD. degree at Harvard University. For 13 years,

DuBois taught history and economics at Atlanta University. Some of his writings include a collection of essays called "The Souls of Black Folk," in 1903; *"Black Reconstruction in America," 1935.* DuBois relocated to Ghana, West Africa where he died, and was buried in 1963.

Gandhi, Mohandas Karamchand (1869 - 1948) Gandhi was a great Indian leader and a world class philosopher. He was a lawyer who gave up western ways to fight for independence for India. He practiced 'Satyagraha' meaning non-violent resistance in his dealings with the British government. He was called 'Mahatma' (great souled). Gandhi was assassinated January 30, 1948 by a Hindu. He is popularly called Mahatma Gandhi.

Garvey, Marcus Mosiah (1887 - 1940), African nationalist leader, was born August 17, 1887, in St. Ann's Bay, Jamaica, British West Indies. He lived briefly in London where he met some Africans from the continent. Later, he returned to Jamaica where he founded the Negro Improvement Association (UNIA). Garvey's message to all African peoples is chiefly a restoration of their self-respect through pride in their glorious past on the one hand; an assurance of a brilliant future through African-owned and African-controlled enterprises. His message was on race pride. He organized the back-to-Africa movement which is still powerful among African Americans, although in a spiritual rather than practical sense.

King James 1 (1566-1625) Became King of England in 1603 and reigned until 1625. He was the son of Lord Darnley and Mary Queen of Scots. He supported the idea of the divine right of kings. His reign marked the beginning of colonial development in North America. It was said of him that he was so knowledgeable he could criticize a theory, but he was a poor

Notes

judge of people.

King, Martin Luther Jr. (1929 - 1968) American clergyman, philosopher and civil rights leader. Dr. King won the Nobel Prize for Peace in 1964. He is probably the greatest orator America has ever produced. Dr. King was assassinated in 1968. He is fondly remembered for his civil rights leadership. His march on Washington, District of Columbia, and his famous speech, ' I HAVE A DREAM' are eloquent testimonies to his greatness as a philosopher. Dr. King practiced what he preached.

Machiavelli, Niccolo (1469-1527) Italian author and statesman who was born in Florence in 1469. Machiavelli is generally remembered for his very unique book 'The Prince' in which he described the activities of a 'successful' ruler.

Malan, Daniel Francois (1874-1959) Prime Minister and leader of the Nationalist Party of the Union of South Africa (1948-54) Malan was a determined advocate of apartheid.

Malcolm X (1925 - 1965) was born in Omaha, Nebraska, May 19, 1925. He was born as Malcolm Little. He attended school but dropped out in eighth grade. Malcolm moved to Boston and became involved in drugs and crime. He spent the years 1946 through 1952 in prison, but became converted to Islam by the Honorable Elijah Muhammad. Malcolm changed his last name to X, signifying an ex-smoker, ex-drinker, ex-Christian, ex-slave. Malcolm was assassinated in 1965, but his martyrdom and ideas and speeches have contributed to the development of African American nationalist ideology on the one hand, and the rise of the 'Black Power' movement of the late 1960's on the other. Like Socrates, he wrote nothing by himself, but there is a large body of literature on him today.

Mandela, Nelson: Nelson Mandela, 73, is currently the leader of the African National Congress (A.N.C.). He was a victim of oppression at the hands of the minority government of South Africa. His long imprisonment of 28 years drew protests against apartheid in every part of the world.

Marx, Karl (1818-1883) German social philosopher and radical thinker. He is the chief theorist of modern socialism. Marx's idea of social change is one of a revolution in which the working class peoples rise against the owners of industries.

Muhammad, Elijah (1897 - 1975), American "Black Muslim" leader, was born Elijah Poole, October 10, 1897, near Sandersville, Georgia. He was one of 13 children born to a Baptist preacher who ran a circuit. He was educated to the fourth grade when he dropped out. In 1923, he moved his family to Detroit, Michigan, and worked there in industrial plants. Elijah seemed to be on public assistance between 1929 and 1931. Elijah met Wali Farad, a Muslim preacher in 1931, and that meeting marked the turning point in his life. He changed Elijah's slave name, "Poole" and substituted "Muhammad." The Honorable Elijah Muhammad's philosophy of self-help for Black Muslims can be seen everywhere in the United States today.

Nkrumah, Kwame (1909 - 1972) Nkrumah became the first President of independent Ghana, a west African State that he had fought hard for for years. Ghana (formerly Gold Coast) was a former British colony. Nkrumah was educated in Catholic mission schools and Achimota College. He later moved to the United States of America to continue his education in 1935. He founded an organization - African Student Organization of the United States and Canada. In 1945, Nkrumah went to England to organize the Pan-African

Notes

Congress. Nkrumah was ousted in a military coup in February 1967. He died in exile in 1972.

Nyerere, Julius Kambarage (1922 -   ). Nyerere was Tanzania's first president of the United Republic of Tanzania. He was baptized a Catholic at 20, and went abroad to study history and political economy. He was the first Tanzanian to attend a British university. Nyerere formulated a type of African socialism built around the term "ujamaa" (Swahili for 'familyhood'). His philosophical ideas are contained in his writings, some of which are: 'African Socialism,' in 1961; 'Freedom and Development,' 1973.

Plato (427 - 347 B.C.) was a Greek philosopher: one of the greatest thinkers of all time. Plato's parents were well-to-do. Plato studied philosophy under Socrates. He later founded a school - the *Academy* where he taught philosophy for the rest of his life.

Reagan, Ronald (born in 1911) was the 40th President of the United States from 1981 to 1989. Earlier, he was governor of the State of California from 1967 to 1974. Reagan was a conservative to the core. The Reagan presidency will be remembered in American history for social, economic, and political 'firsts'. Regan took office in 1980 with the war cry "Communism must be eliminated from the face of the Earth!"

Socrates (469 - 399 B.C.) was a native of Athens. He studied philosophy under teachers in Egypt and went back to teach wisdom to his people. Socrates taught by a system of question and answer. One answer led to another question. Socrates was condemned to death for teaching young men to think. Socrates never wrote anything, but his ideas can be found in the writings of Aristotle and Plato, to name a few.

Index

A

a good name 21
a will 40
abomination 57
accept instruction 21
Action 47, 68
adultery 36
advice 21
Agreements 68
Ambition's gate 47
American dilemma 77
American Dream 77
ancestry 74
ants 18
anxiety 75
apartheid 69, 83
appetite 52
appointment 17
arithmetic 68
attitude 81

B

bad credit 68
bad worker 68
barrels 34
battle 18
beam 23
beating about the bush 18
Beauties 47
beware 74
bird in the hand 34
blacksmith 74
bloom and gloom 75
books 55
born to be leaders 39
borrower 22
Butterflies 34
buttocks 20

C

calabash 59
cannot be false 26
carpet of history 81
cause 76
change 78
Charity 34
chicken 16
child 37
childhood 56
common characteristics 81
Communication 69
community 57
concern 37
confidence 54
consequence 76
consumer 36, 74
content of speech 55
cooks 39
cooperation 55
cost 79
country 81
cowards 48
crawl 18
credit 69
credit system 78
Crimean War 78, 83
curiosity 34, 69

D

danger 16
deaf ear 79
death 48
democracy 62
digest 81
disappointment 17
disaster 18
disease 78
divide 78
division of labor 78
dollars 23
door 23
dunghill 16

E

earthworm 80
elephant 16
enemies 59

Index

England 75
entertaining some angels 22
environment 74
evil 37
evil communications 36
excess 71
exchange 49, 73
exhausted 16
expression 77
eye 60

F

fair tresses 49
fair weather friends 17
familiarity 49
fatigue 79
fish 74
five senses 26
forgive 80
free economy 36
freedom of thought 71

G

gentleman 46
glass-house 24
glories 78
gold locket 20
good character 49
gourd 34
governments 77
gratitude 49
greatness 77
grumble and complain 54
guest-chamber 46

H

habit of reading 50
hawk 78
healer 39
health 36
heaven 49
help 50
house and wealth 49
human victim 24

I

ideas 50
identity 27
impatient person 40
inheritance 34
instruction 18
intelligently 56
invention 36
island 54

J

jealousy and anger 52
joy 54

K

knowledge 52

L

lack 18
lamp 82
largest room 56
late 16
law 56
lazy person 54
leadership 20
learning 52
lender 22
life 18
light and darkness 21
logic 36

M

Machiavelli 53
make new friends 36
Malan 77, 86
Mandela 77, 87
manure 73
market economy 22
market-place 20
Marx 77
maturity 53
meal 36
meanness 76
mental fight 50

mental laziness 76
mice 37
mind your own business 21
minister 21
mistake 52
money 53
morning 53
Mother 36
mouth 56
mutual respect 74

N

nasty 53
nature 75
necessities 21
needle 56
needs 53
nose 17
nourishing 21
number 78

O

Obedience 22
observations 81
obstacle 46
Once bitten 54
Opportunity 36
oppressor 36
organization 69
others' eyebrows 27
Over-mighty 76
overheats 75

P

pain 82
parachutes 53
pen 56
pennies 23
people of good breeding 57
perish 18
personalities 79
Pierian spring 46
piper 56
play 48
Pleasant thoughts 55
Politics 55

political animals 77
poor and happy 75
portion 68
pound of flesh 27
poverty 39
Preparation 37
Prevention 55
prison 37
prisoner 60
prosperity 52
prosperous 80
protect another
  person's head 22
Punctuality 55

Q

quarrelling 17
Quitters 55

R

Reagan 77, 88
reasoned like a child 80
regret 53
Repetition 55
resources 76
ripe apples 39
robust 49, 76
rolling stone 46
roof on fire 22
roots 59
rulers and the ruled 57
run 16
running brook 74

S

sacrifice 22
scarce 81
season 71
secret 68
secret ally 74
secret door to success 24
Seeing 37
Self-reverence 37
sellers and buyers 76
shame 53
shelter 18

91

Index

shoulder 18
Similarity in habits 55
sinking ship 55
skills 52
sluggard 18
small universe 40
smoker 46
social class 48
sparrows 37
spendthrift 16
Spiritual Awareness 26
spoon-fed 73
stage 39
star 16
successful people 24
suffering 48
Supervision 77
survive 60
sweat 75
sweetheart 80
sweetness of cooperation 24
sword 59

T

tame 81
tamed mind 47
task 20, 24
Taxes 56
teachers 56
teaching 18
technology 20, 24
temptation 27
the blind 48
thief 57
thoughts and tongue 24
time 20, 24
time to work 24
tough 79
transforming 21
trouble 17
troublesome person 47
Truth 59
try 20
turbulent sea 39
Two wrongs 59
Tyranny 59

U

Uncontrolled desires 59
Unequal combinations 39
Unity 39
Unrequited love 59
Untrained and
 intractable children 60

V

victories 76
vision 18
voice 78
voting 56

W

Wars 60
watch 50
wicked person 34
wisdom 21, 23, 62
wise 16
wisest fool 57
women's equality 46